Tenor Volume 1
Revised Edition

THE SINGERS MUSICAL THEATRE ANTHOLOGY

A collection of songs from the musical stage, categorized by voice type. The selections are presented in their authentic settings, excerpted from the original vocal scores.

ISBN 0-88188-549-5

D1210234

7777 W. BLUEMOUND RD. P.O. BOX 13819 MILWAUKEE, WI 53213

Visit Hal Leonard Online at
www.halleonard.com

Foreword

The Singer's Musical Theatre Anthology is the most comprehensive series of its kind ever to appear in print. Its unique perspective is in looking at the field of musical theatre in terms of vocal literature. One of the prime parameters in choosing the songs for this series was that they should all be, in some way, particularly vocally gratifying.

Many of the songs included here are very familiar to us, yet we seldom see them printed as they were originally written and performed. The long tradition in sheet music throughout this century has been to adapt a song in several ways to conform to a format which makes it accessible to the average pianist. This type of arrangement is what one finds in vocal selections, or in any piano/vocal collection of show music. These sheet arrangements serve their purpose very well, but aren't really the best performing editions for a singer. In contrast, the selections in this series have been excerpted from the original vocal scores. One of the many benefits of this is a much more satisfying piano accompaniment. In addition, many songs here have never been available separately from the full vocal scores.

In some cases, a song has required some adaptation in order to be excerpted from a show's vocal score. The practice of performing arias as removed from their operatic context gives many precedents for making such adjustments. In many ways, one could view this anthology as a "performing edition." Significant editorial adjustments are indicated by footnotes in some instances.

The original keys of this literature (which are used here) can give important information to a singer about the nature of a song and how it should sound, and in most cases they will work very well for most singers. But, unlike opera, these original keys do not necessarily need to be reverently maintained. With some musical theatre literature, a singer should not rule out transposing a song up or down for vocal comfort.

There is certainly no codified system for classifying theatre music as to voice type. With some roles the classification is obvious. With others there is a good deal of ambiguity. As a result, a particular singer might find suitable literature in this anthology in both volumes of his/her gender.

Any performer of these songs will benefit greatly by a careful study of the show and role from which any given song is taken. This type of approach is taken for granted with an actor preparing a monologue or an opera singer preparing an aria. But because much theatre music has been the popular music of its time, we sometimes easily lose awareness of its dramatic context.

The selections in **The Singer's Musical Theatre Anthology** will certainly be significant additions to a singer's repertory, but no anthology can include every wonderful song. There is a vast body of literature, some of it virtually unknown, waiting to be discovered and brought to life.

The Revised Edition adds four attractive songs to Tenor Volume 1: "King Herod's Song," "A Wand'ring Minstrel I," "Seeing Is Believing" and "Johanna." The last was previously in the Baritone/Bass Volume 1 because the range of the song suits a lyric baritone. However, since Anthony is a tenor role, I've been persuaded this is the more appropriate volume for "Johanna," despite its rather low tessitura.

Richard Walters, editor

THE SINGER'S MUSICAL THEATRE ANTHOLOGY
Tenor

Contents

ABOUT THE SHOWS

The material in this section is by Stanley Green, Richard Walters, and Robert Viagas,
some of which was previously published elsewhere.

ALLEGRO

MUSIC: Richard Rodgers
LYRICS AND BOOK: Oscar Hammerstein II
DIRECTOR AND CHOREOGRAPHER: Agnes de Mille
OPENED: 10/10/47, New York; a run of 315 performances

Allegro was the third Rodgers and Hammerstein musical on Broadway and the first with a story that had not been based on a previous source. It was a particularly ambitious undertaking, with its theme of the corrupting effect of big institutions told through the life of a doctor, Joseph Taylor, Jr. (John Battles), from his birth in a small American town to his thirty-fifth year. Joe grows up, goes to school, marries a local belle (Roberta Jonay), joins the staff of a large Chicago hospital that panders to wealthy patients, discovers that his wife is unfaithful, and, in the end, returns to his home town with his adoring nurse (Lisa Kirk) to dedicate himself to healing the sick and helping the needy. One innovation in the musical was the use of a Greek chorus to comment on the action and sing directly to the actors and the audience.

ASPECTS OF LOVE

MUSIC: Andrew Lloyd Webber
LYRICS: Don Black and Charles Hart
BOOK: Andrew Lloyd Webber
DIRECTOR: Trevor Nunn
CHOREOGRAPHER: Gillian Lynne
OPENED: 4/8/90, New York; a run of 377 performances

The musical is based on an autobiographical novel by David Garnett, a nephew of Virginia Woolf's. While certainly not an outright failure by most standards, *Aspects* remains (as of 2/00) the least successful of Andrew Lloyd Webber's musicals on Broadway. The show had an intimate production style, with orchestrations that threw out the brass in favor of a chamber music sound. The show follows a group of characters over nearly two decades of interweaving relationships. The story begins with a 17-year-old boy who conceives an infatuation with an actress in her mid-20s. The actress already has an older lover, and he has a daughter, and along the way almost everyone winds up in love with, or broken-hearted by, all the others. The plot is emotionally complex, as are the characters and their relationships. Early in the show, when it appears that the young man has successfully persuaded his goddess to run away with him for a tryst, he sings the triumphant "Seeing Is Believing."

THE BOYS FROM SYRACUSE

MUSIC: Richard Rodgers
LYRICS: Lorenz Hart
BOOK: George Abbott
DIRECTOR: George Abbott
CHOREOGRAPHER: George Balanchine
OPENED: 11/23/38, New York; a run of 235 performances

The idea for *The Boys from Syracuse* began when Rodgers and Hart, while working on another show, were discussing the fact that no one had yet done a musical based on a play by Shakespeare. Their obvious choice was *The Comedy of Errors* chiefly because Lorenz Hart's brother Teddy Hart was always being confused with another comic actor, Jimmy Savo. Set in Ephesus in ancient Asia Minor, the ribald tale concerns the efforts of two boys from Syracuse, Antipholus and his servant Dromio (Eddie Albert and Jimmy Savo) to find their long-lost twins, also named Antipholus and Dromio (Ronald Graham and Teddy Hart). Complications arise when the wives of the Ephesians, Adriana (Muriel Angelus) and her servant Luce (Wynn Murray), mistake the two strangers for their husbands. A highly successful Off-Broadway revival of *The Boys from Syracuse* was presented in 1963 and ran for 502 performances. The movie version, which RKO-Radio released in 1940, starred Allan Jones and Joe Penner (both in dual roles). It was directed by A. Edward Sutherland.

CABARET

MUSIC: John Kander
LYRICS: Fred Ebb
BOOK: Joe Masteroff
DIRECTOR: Harold Prince
CHOREOGRAPHER: Ron Field
OPENED: 11/20/66, New York, for a run of 1,165 performances

This moody musical captures the morally corrupt world of Berlin's demimonde just as the Nazis were coming to power. American writer Cliff Bradshaw moves in with Sally Bowles, the hedonistic star singer at a seedy night-club. Soon, he comes to see all of Germany through the dark lens of that increasingly menacing cabaret, which is ruled over by a ghostly Emcee.

CAN-CAN

MUSIC AND LYRICS: Cole Porter
BOOK: Abe Burrows
DIRECTOR: Abe Burrows
CHOREOGRAPHER: Michael Kidd
OPENED: 5/7/53, New York, a run of 892 performances

Next to *Kiss Me, Kate, Can-Can* was Cole Porter's most successful Broadway musical. To make sure that his script would be grounded on the true origins of the scandalous dance known as the Can-Can, librettist Abe Burrows traveled to Paris where he studied the records of the courts, the police, and the Chamber of Deputies. In Burrows' story, set in 1893, La Mome Pistache, owner of the Bal du Paradis, is distressed about the investigation of her establishment because of the Can-Can. She uses her wiles to attract the stern Judge Aristide Forestier, who has been appointed to investigate, but they eventually fall in love and Forestier himself takes over the defense and wins acquittal. The musical, originally intended for Carol Channing, starred the French actress Lilo (who sang the hit ballad, "I Love Paris"), but most of the kudos were for dancer Gwen Verson in her first major Broadway role. A film version with a much altered story was made by Twentieth Century-Fox in 1960. Walter Lang directed, and the cast was headed by Frank Sinatra, Shirley MacLaine, Maurice Chevalier and Louis Jourdan.

THE CAT AND THE FIDDLE

MUSIC: Jerome Kern
LYRICS AND BOOK: Otto Harbach
DIRECTOR: José Ruben
CHOREOGRAPHER: Albertina Rasch
OPENED: 10/15/31, New York; a run of 395 performances

Called "A Musical Romance," *The Cat and the Fiddle* is a gentle, intimate mixture of operetta and musical comedy. The story focuses on the relationship between Victor, a serious Romanian composer of operettas, and Shirley, a fun-loving composer of upbeat American jazz. Kern's clever score reflects the tension and eventual marriage of those two musical styles represented by Victor and Shirley. A movie version was made in 1934, starring Jeanette MacDonald.

CATS

MUSIC: Andrew Lloyd Webber
LYRICS: T.S. Eliot
DIRECTOR: Trevor Nunn
CHOREOGRAPHER: Gillian Lynne
OPENED: London, 5/11/81; New York, 10/7/82; a run of 7,485 performances

Cats opened at the New London Theatre, on May 11, 1981, and, at this writing is still playing there. Charged with energy, flair and imagination, this feline fantasy has proven to be equally successful on Broadway where it is even more of an environmental experience than in the West End. With the entire Winter Garden Theatre transformed into one enormous junkyard, a theatregoer is confronted with such unexpected sights as outsized garbage objects spilling into the audience, the elimination of the proscenium arch, and a ceiling that has been lowered and transformed into a twinkling canopy suggesting both cats' eyes and stars. Adapted from T.S. Eliot's collection of poems, *Old Possum's Book of Practical Cats*, the song-and-dance spectacle introduces such whimsical characters as the mysterious Mr. Mistoffolees, the patriarchal Old Deuteronomy, Skimbleshanks the Railway Cat, and Jennyanydots, the Old Gumbie Cat who sits all day and becomes active only at night. The musical's song hit, "Memory," is sung by Grizabela, the faded Glamour Cat, who, at the evening's end, ascends to the cats' heaven known as the Heaviside Layer.

CELEBRATION

MUSIC: Harvey Schmidt
LYRICS AND BOOK: Tom Jones
DIRECTOR: Tom Jones
OPENED: 1/22/69, New York

The setting is New Year's Eve, that most hopeful of holidays; the theme is of personal renewal and growth. Typically, using a minimum of characters, Schmidt and Jones tell their story with moving simplicity.

COMPANY

MUSIC AND LYRICS: Stephen Sondheim
BOOK: George Furth
DIRECTOR: Harold Prince
CHOREOGRAPHER: Michael Bennett
OPENED: 4/26/70, New York; a run of 706 performances

Company was the first of the Sondheim musicals to have been directed by Harold Prince, and more than any other musical, reflects America in the 1970s. The show is a plotless evening about five affluent couples living in a Manhattan apartment building, and their excessively protective feelings about a charming, but somewhat indifferent bachelor named Bobby. They want to fix him up and see him married, even though it's clear their own marriages are far from perfect. In the end he seems ready to take the plunge. The songs are often very sophisticated, expressing the ambivalent or caustic attitudes of fashionable New Yorkers of the time. Making a connection with another person, the show seems to say, is the key to happiness. An Off-Broadway revue of Sondheim songs also borrowed the song title as its overall title. The show was revived on Broadway in 1998.

DO RE MI

MUSIC: Jule Styne
LYRICS: Betty Comden and Adolph Green
BOOK AND DIRECTION: Garson Kanin
CHOREOGRAPHERS: Marc Breaux and Deedee Wood
OPENED: 12/26/60, New York; a run of 400 performances

A wild satire on the ways in which the underworld muscled in on the jukebox business, *Do Re Mi* was adapted by Kanin from his own novel. With characters reminiscent of the raffish Runyonland denizens of *Guys and Dolls*, the show offered two of Broadway's top clowns of the era: Phil Silvers as a fast-talking would-be big shot, and Nancy Walker as his long-suffering spouse. Nathan Lane and Randy Graff starred in a 1999 "Encores!" revival of the show (recorded by DRG).

FANNY

MUSIC AND LYRICS: Harold Rome
BOOK: S.N. Behrman and Joshua Logan
DIRECTOR: Joshua Logan
CHOREOGRAPHER: Helen Tamiris
OPENED: 11/4/54, New York, a run of 888 perfomances

Marcel Pagnol's French film trilogy, *Marius*, *Fanny*, and *Cesar* were combined into one tale as the basis for *Fanny*, the musical. Marseilles is the setting for the intricate plot. It is a soaring, emotional score, well tailored for the talents of a performer such as Ezio Pinza, an opera star who headed the original cast. A film version of the Broadway *Fanny* was made in 1960, starring Leslie Caron, Maurice Chevalier and Charles Boyer; however no songs from the musical were included.

FINIAN'S RAINBOW

MUSIC: Burton Lane
BOOK: E.Y. Harburg and Fred Saidy
LYRICS: E.Y. Harburg
DIRECTOR: Bretaigne Windust
CHOREOGRAPHER: Michael Kidd
OPENED: 1/10/47, New York; a run of 725 performances

Finian's Rainbow evolved out of co-librettist E.Y. Harburg's desire to satirize an economic system that requires gold reserves to be buried in the ground at Fort Knox. This led to the idea of leprechauns and their crock of gold that, according to legend, could grant three wishes. The story takes place in Rainbow Valley, Missitucky, and involves Finian McLonergan (Albert Sharpe), an Irish immigrant, and his efforts to bury a crock of gold which, he is sure, will grow and make him rich. Also involved are Og (David Wayne), a leprechaun from whom the crock has been stolen, Finian's daughter Sharon (Ella Logan), who dreams wistfully of Glocca Morra, and Woody Mahoney (Donald Richards), a labor organizer who blames that "Old Devil Moon" for the way he feels about Sharon. In the 1968 Warner Bros. adaptation, Fred Astaire played Finian, Petula Clark was his daughter, and Tommy Steele was the leprechaun. The director was Francis Coppola.

FLOWER DRUM SONG

MUSIC: Richard Rodgers
LYRICS: Oscar Hammerstein II
BOOK: Oscar Hammerstein II and Joseph Fields
DIRECTOR: Gene Kelly
CHOREOGRAPHER: Carol Haney
OPENED: 12/1/58, New York; a run of 600 performances

It was librettist Joseph Fields who first secured the rights to C.Y. Lee's novel and then approached Rodgers and Hammerstein to join him as collaborators. To dramatize the conflict between traditionalist older Chinese-Americans living in San Francisco and their thoroughly Americanized offspring, the musical tells the story of Mei Li, a timid "picture bride" from China, who arrives to fulfill her contract to marry nightclub owner Sammy Fong. Sammy, however, prefers dancer Linda Low. The problem is resolved when Sammy's friend Wang Ta discovers that Mei Li really is the bride for him.

A FUNNY THING HAPPENED ON THE WAY TO THE FORUM

MUSIC AND LYRICS: Stephen Sondheim
BOOK: Burt Shevelove and Larry Gelbart
DIRECTOR: George Abbott
CHOREOGRAPHER: Jack Cole
OPENED: 5/8/62, New York; a run of 555 performances

Full of sight gags, pratfalls, mistaken identity, leggy girls, and other familiar vaudeville ingredients, this was a bawdy, farcical, pellmell musical whose likes have seldom been seen on Broadway. Originally intended as a vehicle first for Phil Silvers and then for Milton Berle, *A Funny Thing Happened on the Way to the Forum* opened on Broadway with Zero Mostel as Pseudolus the slave, who is forced to go through a series of mad-cap adventures before being allowed his freedom. Though the show was a hit, things had not looked very promising during the pre-Broadway tryout, and director Jerome Robbins was called in. The most important change: beginning the musical with the song "Comedy Tonight," which set the right mood for the wacky doings that followed. To come up with a script, the librettists researched all twenty-one surviving comedies by the Roman playwright Plautus (254–184 BC), then wrote an original book incorporating such typical Plautus characters as the conniving servants, the lascivious master, the domineering mistress, the officious warrior, the simple-minded hero (called Hero), and the senile old man. One situation, regarding the senile old man who is kept from entering his house because he believes it is haunted, was, in truth, originally discovered in a play titled *Mostellaria*. In 1972, Phil Silvers at last got his chance to appear as Pseudolus in a well-received revival whose run was curtailed by the star's illness. Both Mostel (as Pseudolus) and Silvers (as Marcus Lycus) were in the 1966 United Artists screen version, along with Jack Gilford and Buster Keaton. Richard Lester was the director. The Broadway revival of 1997 starred Nathan Lane as Pseudolus; the role was later played by Whoopi Goldberg, among others.

GYPSY

MUSIC: Jule Styne
LYRICS: Stephen Sondheim
BOOK: Arthur Laurents
DIRECTOR AND CHOREOGRAPHER: Jerome Robbins
OPENED: 5/21/59, New York; a run of 702 performances

Written for Ethel Merman, who gave the performance of her career as Gypsy Rose Lee's ruthless, domineering mother, *Gypsy* is one of the great scores in the mature musical comedy tradition. The idea for the musical began with producer David Merrick, who needed to read only one chapter in Miss Lee's autobiography to convince him of its stage potential. Originally, Stephen Sondheim was to have supplied the music as well as the lyrics, but Miss Merman, who had just come from a lukewarm production on Broadway, wanted the more experienced Jule Styne. In the story, Mama Rose is determined to escape from her humdrum life by pushing the vaudeville career of her daughter June. After June runs away to get married, Mama focuses all her attention on her other daughter, the previously neglected Louise. As vaudeville declines, so do their fortunes, until an accidental booking at a burlesque theatre, and Louise's ad-libbed striptease, turns Louise into a star, the legendary Gypsy Rose Lee. Rose achieves a version of her dream, but suffers a breakdown when she realizes that she is no longer needed in her daughter's career. Several major stars have played Mama Rose. Rosalind Russell won the role in the 1962 film. Angela Lansbury toplined a successful mid 1970s revival in London and New York in the mid 1970s. Tyne Daly gave the role a new spin in 1989. Bette Midler brought the show to a wider audience in a mid 1990s TV adaptation.

JESUS CHRIST SUPERSTAR

MUSIC: Andrew Lloyd Webber
LYRICS: Tim Rice
DIRECTOR: Tom O'Horgan
OPENED: 10/12/71, New York; a run of 711 performances

This was the show that boosted Andrew Lloyd Webber and Tim Rice to international prominence, a musical that presumed to make a Broadway musical star out of Jesus and to make the last weeks of his life sing and dance. Though *Superstar* was conceived as a theatre piece, Lloyd Webber and Rice couldn't convince producers that their "rock opera" had the slightest chance. Instead, they recorded it as a rock album, and it immediately became a smash hit, the first such "concept album" of a show in development. Concert tours of the show followed, and soon producers didn't need any more convincing that this would fly in the theatre. Despite some mixed press about the production, and some outcries and picketing from religious groups, the piece had its appeal, particularly among the young. The show broke all records in London, and pioneered the concept of a "through-sung" opera-like musical, which had its effect on shows to follow, including *Evita, Cats, Les Misérables, Miss Saigon* and *The Phantom of the Opera.* "King Herod's Song" turns Herod's taunting of the imprisoned Jesus into a campy vaudeville two-beat. A 1974 film followed. A Broadway revival opened in the year 2000.

KISMET

MUSIC AND LYRICS: Robert Wright and George Forrest (Based on music by Alexander Borodin)
BOOK: Charles Lederer and Luther Davis
DIRECTOR: Albert Marre
CHOREOGRAPHER: Jack Cole
OPENED: 12/3/53, New York; a run of 583 performances

The story of *Kismet* was adapted from Edward Knoblock's play, first presented in New York in 1911 as a vehicle for Otis Skinner. The music of *Kismet* was adapted from themes by Alexander Borodin first heard in such works as the "Polovetzian Dances," ("He's in Love," "Stranger in Paradise") and in "Steppes of Central Asia," ("Sands of Time"). The action of the musical occurs within a twenty-four hour period, in and around ancient Baghdad. A Public Poet (Alfred Drake) assumes the identity of Hajj the beggar and gets into all sorts of Arabian Nights adventures. His schemes get him elevated to the position of emir of Baghdad and get his beautiful daughter Marsinah (Doretta Morrow) wed to the handsome young Caliph (Richard Kiley). The film version was made by MGM in 1955, with Howard Keel as Hajj. Vincente Minnelli directed.

LOST IN THE STARS

MUSIC: Kurt Weill
LYRICS AND BOOK: Maxwell Anderson
DIRECTOR: Rouben Mamoulian
OPENED: 10/30/49, New York; a run of 273 performances

Kurt Weill's final Broadway musical (his second in collaboration with Maxwell Anderson) was written to convey "a message of hope that people, through a personal approach, will solve whatever racial problems that exist." In the idealistic story, adapted from Alan Paton's *Cry, the Beloved Country*, the action is set in and around Johannesburg, South Africa. Absalom Kumalo, the errant son of a black minister, Stephen Kumalo, accidentally kills a white man in a robbery attempt and is condemned to hang. The tragedy, however, leads to a sympathetic bond between Stephen and James Jarvis, the dead man's father, which gives some indication that understanding between the races can be achieved in the land of apartheid. A newer version, presented by Ely Landau's American Film theatre, was shown in 1974 with a cast headed by Brock Peters and Melba Moore.

ME AND JULIET

MUSIC: Richard Rodgers
LYRICS: Oscar Hammerstein II
BOOK: Blake Edwards
DIRECTOR: George Abbott
CHOREOGRAPHER: Robert Alton
OPENED: 5/28/53, New York; a run of 358 performances

Me and Juliet was Rodgers and Hammerstein's Valentine to show business, with its action—in *Kiss Me, Kate* style—taking place both backstage in a theatre and onstage during the performance of a play. Here, the tale concerns a romance between a singer in the chorus and the assistant stage manager, whose newfound bliss is seriously threatened by the jealous electrician. A comic subplot involves the stage manager and the principal dancer.

THE MIKADO

MUSIC: Arthur Sullivan
LIBRETTO: W.S. Gilbert
OPENED: March 14, 1885, London

Into the town of Titipu rushes Nanki-Poo, who introduces himself to the populace before stating his business: he seeks news of Yum-Yum, his true love. Alas, she is to be married that very afternoon to Ko-Ko, the Lord High Executioner. Ko-Ko enters to general acclaim. He has no intention of executing anyone, ever, for in truth he is next in line for the chopping block. Unfortunately for him, that day has arrived, for word comes from the Mikado, the emperor of Japan, that someone must be executed, and soon. Ko-Ko finds a willing subject in Nanki-Poo, who, contemplating suicide rather than life without Yum-Yum, agrees to be beheaded instead, under the condition that he first be allowed a month as Yum-Yum's husband. The young lovers wed, and Ko-Ko ultimately agrees to pretend the execution has taken place without actually performing it. All seems well until the Mikado himself appears, accompanied by the spinster Katisha. She's long had her sights set on Nanki-Poo, who it turns out is no troubadour, but the Mikado's son. The only way to avert her wrath is for Ko-Ko to woo her, which, reluctantly, he does, and marry her himself. In this lampoon of corruption in government, even underhanded officials can eventually bring about a happy ending.

MY FAIR LADY

MUSIC: Frederick Loewe
LYRICS AND BOOK: Alan Jay Lerner
DIRECTOR: Moss Hart
CHOREOGRAPHER: Hanya Holm
OPENED: 3/15/56, New York; a run of 2,717 performances

The most celebrated musical of the 1950s began as an idea of Hungarian film producer Gabriel Pascal, who devoted the last two years of his life trying to find writers to adapt George Bernard Shaw's play, *Pygmalion*, into a stage musical. The team of Lerner and Loewe also saw the possibilities, particularly when they realized that they could use most of the original dialogue and simply expand the action to include scenes at the Ascot Races and Embassy Ball. They were also scrupulous in maintaining the Shavian flavor in their songs, most apparent in such pieces as "Get Me to the Church on Time," "Why Can't the English?," "Show Me" and "Without You." Shaw was concerned that British society had become so stratified and segregated that different classes had developed their own separate accents. His concern was dramatized in the story of Eliza Doolittle (originated in the musical by Julie Andrews), a scruffy flower seller in London's Covent Garden, who takes speech lessons from Prof. Henry Higgins (Rex Harrison) so that she might qualify for the position of a florist in a shop. Eliza succeeds so well that she outgrows her social station and, in a development added by librettist Lerner, even makes Higgins fall in love with her. *My Fair Lady* became the longest running production in Broadway history, and remained so for nearly seven years. Three major revivals have been mounted in New York since then. In 1976, the musical ran for 377 performance with Ian Richardson and Christine Andreas as Higgins and Eliza. Harrison returned in 1981 with Nancy Ringham as his Fair Lady. Richard Chamberlain and Melissa Errico brought a radically redesigned version to Broadway in 1993. Harrison and Audrey Hepburn (whose singing was dubbed by Marni Nixon) were seen in the 1964 Warner Bros. movie version, which was directed by George Cukor.

OKLAHOMA!

MUSIC: Richard Rodgers
LYRICS AND BOOK: Oscar Hammerstein II
DIRECTOR: Rouben Mamoulian
CHOREOGRAPHER: Agnes de Mille
OPENED: 3/31/43, New York; a run of 2,212 performances

There are many reasons why *Oklahoma!* is a recognized landmark in the history of American musical theatre. In the initial collaboration between Richard Rodgers and Oscar Hammerstein II, it not only expertly fused the major elements in the production—story, songs and dances— it also utilized dream ballets to reveal hidden desires and fears of the principals. In addition, the musical, based on Lynn Riggs' play, *Green Grow the Lilacs*, was the first with a book that honestly depicted the kind of rugged pioneers who had once tilled the land and tended the cattle. Set in Indian Territory soon after the turn of the century, *Oklahoma!* spins a simple tale mostly concerned with whether the decent Curly (Alfred Drake) or the menacing Jud (Howard Da Silva) gets to take Laurey (Joan Roberts) to the box social. Though she chooses Jud in a fit of pique, Laurey really loves Curly and they soon make plans to marry. At their wedding they join in celebrating Oklahoma's impending statehood, then—after Jud is accidentally killed in a fight with Curly—the couple rides off in their surrey with the fringe on top. With its Broadway run of five years, nine months, *Oklahoma!* established a long-run record that it held for fifteen years. It also toured the United States and Canada for over a decade. In 1979, the musical was revived on Broadway with a cast headed by Laurence Guittard and Christine Andreas, and ran for 293 performances. The film version, the first in Todd-AO, was released by Magna in 1955. Gordon MacRae, Shirley Jones and Charlotte Greenwood were in it, and the director was Fred Zinnemann.

ONCE UPON A MATTRESS

MUSIC: Mary Rodgers
BOOK: Jay Thompson, Dean Fuller and Marshall Barer
LYRICS: Marshall Barer
DIRECTOR: George Abbott
CHOREOGRAPHER: Joe Layton
OPENED: 5/11/59, New York; a run of 460 performances

Based on the fairy tale "The Princess and the Pea," the musical tells the story of a domineering queen's search for a true princess suitable for marrying her son, the prince. The test involves sleeping on a pile of mattresses while detecting the uncomfortable presence of a pea at the bottom of the pile. Winnifred passes the test with the aid of a mischievous minstrel. The show is notable as the stage debut of Carol Burnett playing Winnifred. Mary Rodgers, the show's composer, is the daughter of Richard Rodgers.

PAL JOEY

MUSIC: Richard Rodgers
BOOK: John O'Hara
LYRICS: Lorenz Hart
DIRECTOR: George Abbott
CHOREOGRAPHER: Robert Alton
OPENED: 12/25/40, New York; a run of 374 performances

With its heel for a hero, its smoky night-club atmosphere, and its true-to-life charachters, *Pal Joey* was a major breakthrough in bringing about a more adult form of musical theatre. Adapted by John O'Hara from his own *New Yorker* short stories, the show is about Joey Evans, an entertainer at a small Chicago night club, who is attracted to the innocent Linda English, but drops her in favor of a wealthy, middle-aged Vera Simpson. Vera builds a glittering night club, the Chez Joey, for her paramour but she soon grows tired of him, and Joey, at the end, is on his way to other conquests. In his only major Broadway role, Gene Kelly got the chance to sing "I Could Write a Book," and Vivienne Segal, as Vera, introduced "Bewitched." Though it had a respectable run, *Pal Joey* was considered somewhat ahead of its time when it was first produced. A 1952 Broadway revival, with Miss Segal repeating her original role and Harold Lang as Joey, received a more appreciative reception and went on to a run of 542 performances. In 1957, Columbia made a film version, with George Sidney directing, which starred Frank Sinatra, Kim Novak, and Rita Hayworth.

PIPE DREAM

MUSIC: Richard Rodgers
LYRICS AND BOOK: Oscar Hammerstein II
DIRECTOR: Harold Clurman
CHOREOGRAPHER: Boris Runanin
OPENED: 11/30/55, New York; a run of 246 performances

A Rodgers and Hammerstein musical set in a brothel? Sounds crazy, no? But in John Steinbeck's little village of Cannery Row, they created a collection of soft-centered sinners and sent them about their business in this leisurely paced musical with little conflict. *Pipe Dream* was adapted from John Steinbeck's *Sweet Thursday*, and took a sympathetic look at the inhabitants of skid row in California's Monterey peninsula. The plot is mostly about Doc, a marine biologist, whose romance with a pretty vagrant named Suzy is abetted by Fauna, the warmhearted madam of a local brothel.

ROBERTA

MUSIC: Jerome Kern
LYRICS AND BOOK: Otto Harbach
DIRECTOR: Hassard Short
CHOREOGRAPHER: José Limón
OPENED: 11/18/33, New York; a run of 295 performances

The musical was adapted from Alice Duer Miller's novel *Gowns by Roberta*, but in the end the little plot that remained in the show seems to be a scant framework for some first rate songs. *Roberta* is probably best remembered as the source for its most famous song, "Smoke Gets in Your Eyes." Two film versions were made of the play, the first one in 1953 and starring Irene Dunne, Fred Astaire and Ginger Rogers.

SHENANDOAH

MUSIC: Gary Geld
LYRICS: Peter Udell
BOOK: James Lee Barrett, Peter Udell and Philip Rose (Based on a screenplay by James Lee Barrett)
DIRECTOR: Philip Rose
CHOREOGRAPHER: Robert Tucker
OPENED: 1/7/75, New York; a run of 1,050 performances

Shenandoah is a traditional musical concerned with a strong-willed Virginia widower and his determination to prevent his family from becoming involved in the Civil War. John Cullums' robust performance and the play's old-fashioned morality found favor with Broadway audiences for well over two years.

SOUTH PACIFIC

MUSIC: Richard Rodgers
LYRICS: Oscar Hammerstein II
BOOK: Oscar Hammerstein II and Joshua Logan
DIRECTOR: Joshua Logan
OPENED: 4/7/49, New York; a run of 1,925 performances

South Pacific had the second longest Broadway run of the nine musicals with songs by Richard Rodgers and Oscar Hammerstein II. Director Joshua Logan first urged the partners to adapt a short story, "Fo' Dolla," contained in James Michener's book about World War II, *Tales of the South Pacific*. Rodgers and Hammerstein, however, felt that the story, about Lt. Joe Cable's tender romance with Liat, a Polynesian girl, was a bit too much like *Madame Butterfly*, and they suggested that another story in the collection, "Our Heroine," should provide the main plot. This one was about the unlikely attraction between Nellie Forbush, a naïve Navy nurse from Little Rock, and Emile de Becque, a sophisticated French planter living on a Pacific island. The tales were combined by having Cable and de Becque go on a dangerous mission together behind Japanese lines. Coming just a few years after the war, and featuring several veterans in the cast, the show was enormously resonant with 1949 audiences. But there has not so far been a major Broadway revival. Perhaps because of its daring (for the time) theme of the evils of racial prejudice, it was also the second musical to be awarded the prestigious Pulitzer Prize for Drama. This production was the first of two musicals (the other was *The Sound of Music*) in which Mary Martin, who played Nellie, was seen as a Rodgers and Hammerstein heroine. It also marked the Broadway debut of famed Metropolitan Opera basso, Ezio Pinza, who played de Becque. Mitzi Gaynor and Rossano Brazzi starred in 20th Century-Fox's 1958 film version, also directed by Logan.

STREET SCENE

MUSIC: Kurt Weill
LYRICS: Langston Hughes
BOOK: Elmer Rice
DIRECTOR: Charles Friedman
CHOREOGRAPHER: Anna Sokolow
OPENED: 1/9/47, New York; a run of 148 performances

Kurt Weill persuaded Elmer Rice to write the libretto based on his own Pulitzer Prize-winning play with poet Langston Hughes supplying the powerful and imaginative lyrics. Billed as "a dramatic musical," the blending of drama and music was very close to genuine opera. In fact, the play went on in 1966 to become part of the repertory of the New York City Opera Company. The story deals principally with the brief, star-crossed romance of Sam Kaplan (Brian Sullivan) and Rose Maurrant (Anne Jeffreys) and the tragic consequences of the infidelity of Rose's mother (Polyna Stoska). This plot loosely frames a series of vignettes, each depicting one of the colorful characters inhabiting the seedy tenement of the setting.

SUNDAY IN THE PARK WITH GEORGE

MUSIC AND LYRICS: Stephen Sondheim
BOOK: James Lapine
DIRECTOR: James Lapine
OPENED: 5/2/84, New York; a run of 604 performances

The centerpiece of the ambitious show is George Seurat's great painting "A Sunday Afternoon on the Island of La Grande Jatte." It is an intimate and personal musical concerned with the creative process itself, its obsessions and consequences. The song included in this volume, "Finishing the Hat," shows us George's inner conflict between his undaunted commitment to his work and his love for a woman. The second act of the show deals with the same artistic tensions (plus a few more) in a present day setting. The piece received the Pulitzer Prize for drama in 1985. An adaptation of the Broadway production (starring Mandy Patinkin and Bernadette Peters) was made for television, and has been broadcast several times.

SWEENEY TODD, THE DEMON BARBER OF FLEET STREET

MUSIC AND LYRICS: Stephen Sondheim
BOOK: Hugh Wheeler
DIRECTOR: Harold Prince
OPENED: 3/1/79, New York; a run of 557 performances

Despite the sordidness of its main plot—a half mad, vengeance-obsessed barber in Victorian London slits the throats of his customers whose corpses are then turned into meat pies by his accomplice, Mrs. Lovett—this near-operatic musical is a bold and often brilliant depiction of the cannibalizing effects of the Industrial Revolution. *Sweeney Todd* first appeared on the London stage in 1842 in a play called *A String of Pearls, or The Fiend of Fleet Street*. Other versions followed, the most recent being Christopher Bond's *Sweeney Todd*, produced in 1973, which served as the basis of the musical. Sondheim's masterwork has gained a foothold in the operatic repertory, with prominent productions at Houston and at New York City Opera.

TWO BY TWO

MUSIC: Richard Rodgers
LYRICS: Martin Charnin
BOOK: Peter Stone
DIRECTOR: Joe Layton
OPENED: 1/10/70, New York; a run of 343 performances

After an absence of almost thirty years, Danny Kaye returned to Broadway in a musical based on the legend of Noah and the Ark. Adapted from Clifford Odets' play, *The Flowering Peach*, *Two by Two* dealt primarily with Noah's rejuvenation and his relationship with his wife and family as he undertakes the formidable task that God has commanded. During the run, Kaye suffered a torn ligament in his left leg and was briefly hospitalized. He returned hobbling on a crutch with his leg in a cast, a situation he used as an excuse to depart from the script by cutting up and clowning around. For his third musical following Oscar Hammerstein's death, composer Richard Rodgers joined lyricist Martin Charnin (later to be responsible for *Annie*) to create the melodious score.

WISH YOU WERE HERE

MUSIC AND LYRICS: Harold Rome
BOOK: Arthur Kober and Joshua Logan
DIRECTOR AND CHOREOGRAPHER: Joshua Logan
OPENED: 6/25/52, New York; a run of 598 performances

It was known as the musical with the swimming pool, but *Wish You Were Here* had other things going for it, including a castful of ingratiating performers, a warm and witty score by Harold Rome, and a director who wouldn't stop making improvements even after the Broadway opening (among them were new dances choreographed by Jerome Robbins). The musical was adapted by Arthur Kober and Joshua Logan from Kober's own play, *Having a Wonderful Time*, and was concerned with a group of middle-class New Yorkers trying to make the most of a two-week vacation at an adult summer camp in the mountains.

YOU ARE NEVER AWAY

from *Allegro*

Words by OSCAR HAMMERSTEIN II
Music by RICHARD RODGERS

free. _____ You're the

smile _____ on my face, or a song _____ that I sing! You're a

rain - bow I chase on a morn - ing in spring, You're a

star _____ in the lace of a wild _____ wil - low tree, In the

mf a tempo

mp

green leaf-y lace of a wild wil - low tree! But to - night you're no star, Nor a song that I sing, In my

SEEING IS BELIEVING
from *Aspects of Love*

Music by ANDREW LLOYD WEBBER
Lyrics by DON BLACK and CHARLES HART

train go by, I'll think of us, the night, the sky for-

e - - - ver.

COME WITH ME
from *The Boys from Syracuse*

Words by LORENZ HART
Music by RICHARD RODGERS

Moderately bright - In 2

Come with me where the food is free, Where the land-lord nev-er comes near you. Be a guest in a house of rest, Where the best of fel-lows can cheer

you. There's your own lit-tle room So cool, not too much light, _____ Where you're one man for whom No wife waits up at night. _____ When day ends you have lots of

Much slower - In 2

You nev - er have to fetch the milk Or walk the dog at ear - ly dawn. There's no "get up, you're late for work" While you rest in the pearl-y dawn. You're nev - er bored by pol - i - tics. You're priv - i - leged to miss a row of trag - e - dies by Soph - o - cles And

(sempre stacc.)

di - a - tribes by Cic - e - ro. Your broth - er's wife will nev - er come On

Rubato

Sun - day noon to bring to you Her lit - tle son, who plays the lute, Her

rall.

In tempo

lit - tle girl to sing to you. You can com - mit your lit - tle sins And rel - a - tives won't

simile

fz   *mf*

yell "fie!" You need - n't take that an - nu - al trip To the or - a - cle at

Del-phi. You snore and swear and stretch and yawn In this, your strict-ly male house. The

on-ly way that sin-ners go to heav-en Is in the jail-house.

cresc. *poco* *a* *poco* *f*

Tempo I

Come with me where the food is free, Where the

mf

34

SITTING PRETTY
(THE MONEY SONG)
from *Cabaret*

Lyric by FRED EBB
Music by JOHN KANDER

Frantic (in 2)

M.C.:

My fa - ther needs mon - ey. My un - cle needs mon - ey. My moth - er is thin___ as a reed.___ But me, I'm sit - ting pret - ty.___ I've got all the mon - ey I

lit - tle cous - in Er - ic has his cred - i - tors hys - ter - i - cal, And al - so cous - in Her - man had to

pawn his moth-er's er - mine And my sis - ter and my bro - ther took to hock - ing one an - oth - er

too. But I've got some tal - ents which

build up my bal - ance, So e - ven my bank - er's a -

sis - ter and my broth-er took to hock-ing one an-oth-er too._____ But

I'm not a nin - com - poop, I've got an in - come you

put in the bank to ac - crue._____ Yes,

me, I'm sit - ting pret - ty._____

IF YOU COULD SEE HER

from *Cabaret*

Lyric by FRED EBB
Music by JOHN KANDER

Ad lib.

just a first im-pres-sion, ___ What good's a first im-pres-sion? ___ If you

(ad lib.)

knew her like I do It would change your point of view.

rall.

Cb7(F♯7) arp. (ad lib.)

[Schottische]

If you could see ___ her through my eyes,
How can I speak ___ of her vir - tues?

You would-n't won - der at
I don't know where ___ to be -

all.
gin.

She's clev - er, she's smart, ___ she reads mu - sic,

If you could see ___ her through my eyes,

I guar - an - tee____ you would fall (like I did.) When we're in pub - lic to -
She does - n't smoke____ or drink gin (like I do.) Yet, when we're walk - ing to -

geth - er I hear so - ci - e - ty moan. But
geth - er, They sneer if I'm hold - ing her hand. But

if they could see____ her through my eyes May - be they'd leave____ us a -
if they could see____ her through my eyes May - be they'd all____ un - der -

1.

lone.

I AM IN LOVE
from *Can-Can*

Words and Music by
COLE PORTER

Why this e - la - tion _ Mixed with de - fla - tion?

What ex - plan - a - tion? I _ am in love!

Such con-flict - ing ques - tions ride A - round _ in my brain,

Should I or - der cy - an-ide, Or or - der cham - pagne? _

Oh what is this sud - den jolt? _ I feel like a fright-en'd colt,

cresc.

Just hit by a thun-der-bolt, I ___ am in love.

I knew the odds Were a-gainst me be-fore, I

had no flair For flam-ing de-sire, But

since the Gods ___ Gave me you to a-dore, I may lose but I re-

-fuse to fight the fire! So come and en-light-en my days

A NEW LOVE IS OLD
from *The Cat and the Fiddle*

Music by JEROME KERN
Words by OTTO HARBACH

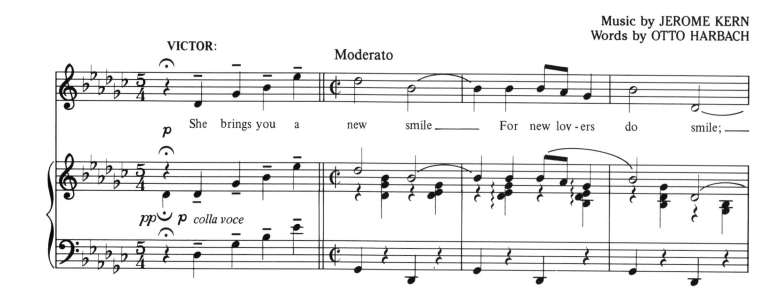

51

She tempts you and you smile; _____ A new love is told. _____ She brings you some new thrills, _____ Some ten-der and true thrills, _____ But af-ter a few thrills _____ Your new love is old. _____

THE BREEZE KISSED YOUR HAIR

from *The Cat and the Fiddle*

Music by JEROME KERN
Words by OTTO HARBACH

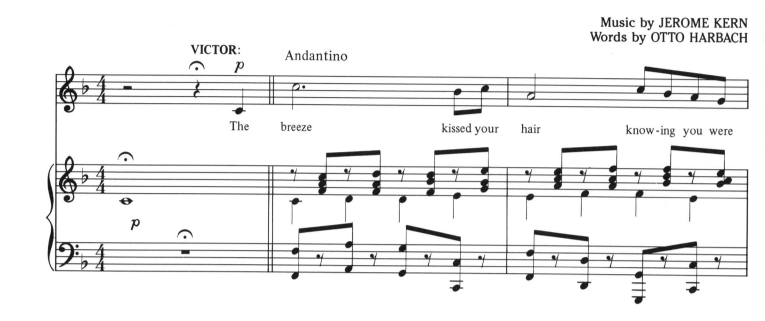

THE BALLAD OF BILLY M'CAW
from *Cats*

Words by T.S. ELIOT
Music by ANDREW LLOYD WEBBER

par - ret, the par - ret named Bil - ly M' Caw, that brought all those folk to the bar. Ah!

freely

colla voce

he was the life of the bar. Of a sat - ta - day night, we was all feel - ing bright, And

a tempo

Li - ly La Rose, the barmaid that was, she'd say 'Bil - ly! Bil - ly M' - Caw! _____ Come

a tempo

give us, come give us a dance on the bar'. And Bil -ly would dance on the bar, and

Bil - ly would dance on the bar. And then we'd feel bal - my, in

each eye a tear, And e - mo - tion would make us all or - der more beer. Li - ly,

she was a girl what had brains in her head; She would-n't have no - think, no

not that much said. If it come to an ar - gu - ment, or a dis - pute, She'd set - tle it off - hand with the

62

BEING ALIVE
from *Company*

Words and Music by
STEPHEN SONDHEIM

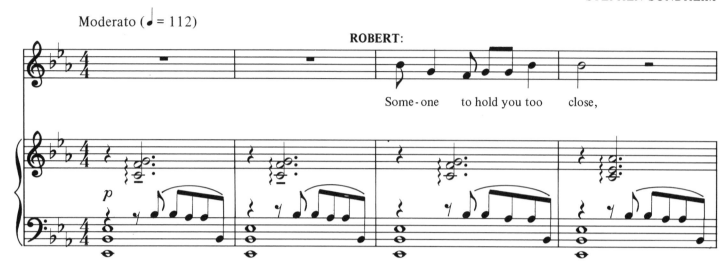

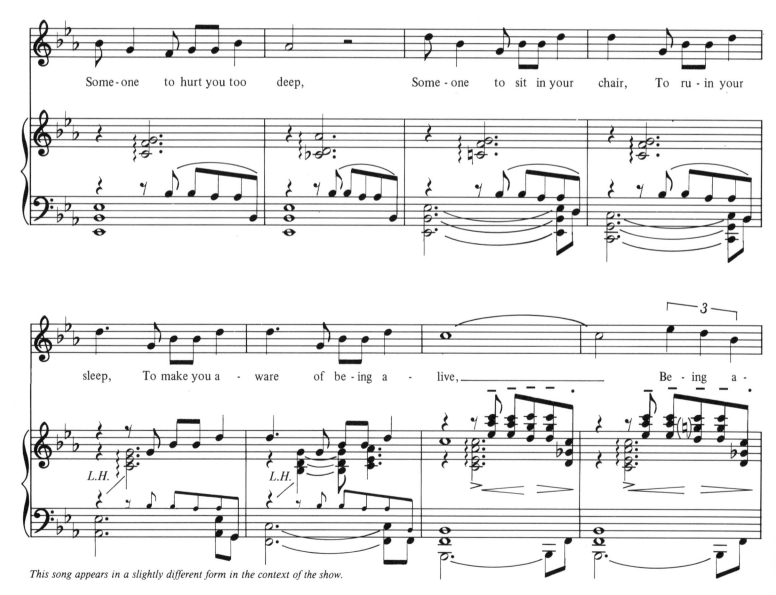

This song appears in a slightly different form in the context of the show.

Some-one you have to let in, Some-one whose feel-ings you spare,

Some-one who like it or not, Will want you to share A lit-tle, a lot, Is be-ing a-

live, _____ Be - ing a - live. _____

Some-one to crowd you with love, Some-one to force you to care.

Some - one to make you come through, Who'll al - ways be there, as fright-ened as you of be-ing a -

live, _____ Be - ing a - live, _____ Be - ing a -

live, _____ Be - ing a - live. _____

Some-bod - y hold me too close,

Some-bod - y hurt me too

68

deep,   Some - bod - y sit in my   chair   And ru - in my

sleep   and make me a - ware   Of be - ing a - live, _____

Be - ing a - live. _____

Some - bod - y need me too   much,   Some - bod - y know me too

well;
Some - bod - y pull me up short
And put me through

hell and give me sup - port
For be - ing a - live.

Make me a - live,
Make me a -

live,
Make me con - fused,
Mock me with

L.H.
(R.H.)

mf

Some-bod-y force me to care. Some-bod-y let me come through, I'll al-ways be

there as fright-ened as you To help us sur-vive_____ Be-ing a-

live,_____ Be-ing a-live,_____ Be-ing a-

live!

L.H.

R.H. *cresc.* *poco a poco*

rit.

ff

sfz *sffz*

8 bassa - - - - - - - - - - -

SOMEONE IS WAITING
from *Company*

Words and Music by
STEPHEN SONDHEIM

FIFTY MILLION YEARS AGO

from *Celebration*

Words by TOM JONES
Music by HARVEY SCHMIDT

With motion

mf

ORPHAN:

Fif - ty mil - lion years a - go,

mp

Some - thing in the sea

simile

Reached a - bove the

wa - ter ea - ger - ly!

Can it be that there's no rea - son why,

When, in spite of all the strife,

And the end - less dy - ing, Life keeps reach - ing

high - er for the sky?

8 bassa -

ff

MAKE SOMEONE HAPPY

from *Do Re Mi*

Words by BETTY COMDEN & ADOLPH GREEN
Music by JULE STYNE

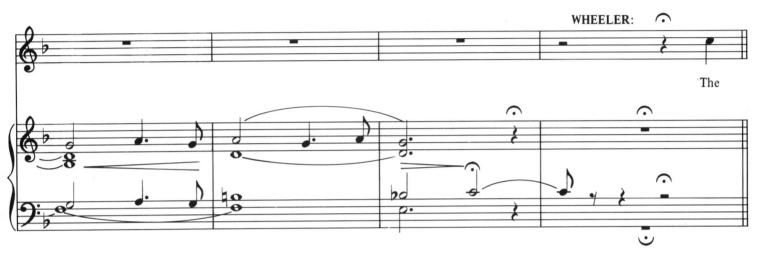

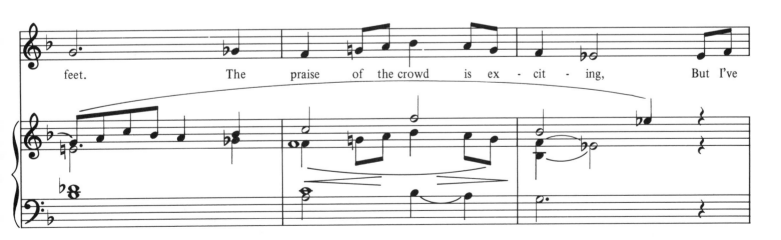

found him, Build your world a - round him.

Make _____ some-one hap - py, Make just one _____

mf

poco rit.

_____ some-one hap - py, And you _____ will be hap - py

p

rall.

Più mosso (in 4)　　　　　Marcato

too. _____

mf　　　　　*f*　　　　　*ff*

FANNY
from *Fanny*

Words and Music by
HAROLD ROME

WHEN I'M NOT NEAR THE GIRL I LOVE

from *Finian's Rainbow*

Words by E.Y. HARBURG
Music by BURTON LANE

slen - der; Long as they've got that gen - der, I

s'rrender. _____ Al - ways I can't re-

fuse 'em; Al - ways my feet pur - sues 'em;

poco accel.

Long as they've got a bo - som, I woo's 'em. _____

I'm con - fess - ing a con - fes - sion _____

_____ and I hope I'm not ver - bose, _____ When

I'm ___ not close to the kiss that I cling to, I cling to, I kiss that's close. ___ As I'm more and more a mor - tal, ___ I am more and more a case. ___ When I'm ___ not fac - ing the face that I fan - cy, I

fan - cy the face I face. _____ For Sha - ron I'm car - in'; ___ But

Su - zan I'm choo-sin', _ I'm faith - ful to who - s'n ___ is here. _____ When

I'm ___ not near ___ the girl ___ I love, ___ I love ___ the girl _____

_____ I'm near.

YOU ARE BEAUTIFUL

from *Flower Drum Song*

Words by OSCAR HAMMERSTEIN II
Music by RICHARD RODGERS

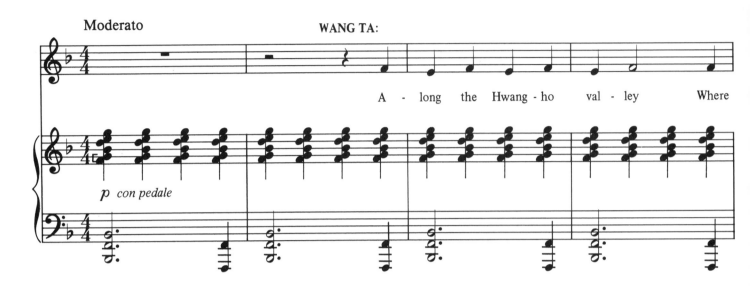

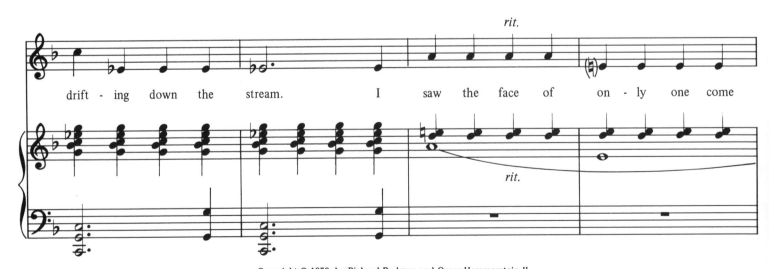

Pass-ing the riv - er shore. You are the girl whose laugh I heard,

Sil - ver and soft and bright; Soft as the fall of lo - tus leaves

Brush - ing the air of night. While your flow - er boat

sailed a - way Gent - ly your eyes looked back on mine,

Clear - ly you heard me say: "You are the girl I will love some

day."

You are the girl whose laugh I heard, Sil - ver and soft and bright;

LOVE, I HEAR
from *A Funny Thing Happened on the Way to the Forum*

Words and Music by
STEPHEN SONDHEIM

Moderately - In 4

Love, I hear,_____ Makes you sigh a lot. Al - so,

love, I hear,_____ Leaves you weak._____

Love, I hear,_____ Makes you blush and turns you ash - en. You

try to speak with pas - sion and squeak, I hear.

know I am, I'm sure__ I mean, I hope I trust__ I pray__ I must__ Be

in! _____ For-

Tempo primo

give me if I shout.____ For-give me if I crow.____ I've

on-ly just found out, And, well, I thought you ought to know.____

ALL I NEED IS THE GIRL

from *Gypsy*

Words by STEPHEN SONDHEIM
Music by JULE STYNE

Moderato ($\frac{}{} = 92$)

TULSA:

Once my ___ clothes were shab-by.

Tail - ors ___ called me "cab-bie". So I ___ took a vow, ___

Said, "This bum - 'll be beau Brum-mell." Now I'm ___ smooth and snap - py,

Now my — tail-or's hap-py. I'm the — cat's me-ow! — My

ward-robe is a wow! — Pa - ris — silk, —

Har-ris — tweed. — There's on - ly one thing — I

A little slower (♩ = 88)

need. — Got my tweed pressed, — Got my

best vest, ___ All I need now ___ is the

girl! _____ Got my striped tie, ___ Got my

hopes high, ___ Got the time and the place And I ___ got rhyth - m,

Now all I need's the girl ___ to go with 'em. If she'll ___ just ap -

pear, We'll __ take this big town __ for a whirl. __

__ And if she'll __ say, "My dar - ling, I'm yours," I'll throw_

__ a - way __ my striped tie __ And my best pressed tweed,_

__ All I real - ly need __ is the girl!

STRANGER IN PARADISE

from *Kismet*

Words and Music by ROBERT WRIGHT and GEORGE FORREST
(Based on themes of A. BORODIN)

stand be - side An an - gel like you.

Più mosso

I saw your face And I as - cend - ed

Out of the com - mon - place In - to the rare!

Some - where in space I hang sus - pend - ed

And tell him that he need be ___ A stran-ger no more.

A tempo

I saw your

Tempo as in first refrain

face ___ And I as-cend -ed ___ Out of the

KING HEROD'S SONG

from *Jesus Christ Superstar*

Words by TIM RICE
Music by ANDREW LLOYD WEBBER

Moderato, ad lib.

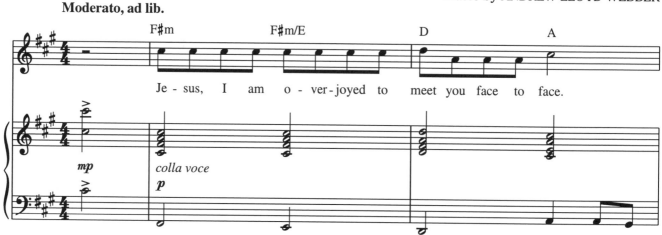

Je - sus, I am o - ver - joyed to meet you face to face.

You've been get - ting quite a name all a - round the place, _ Heal - ing crip - ples,

rais - ing from the dead, And now I un - der - stand you're God, at

120

Moderato, Ragtime style

THE WILD JUSTICE
from *Lost in the Stars*

Words by MAXWELL ANDERSON
Music by KURT WEILL

Moderato assai, quasi sostenuto

LEADER:
noblimente

Have you fished for a fixed star with the lines of its light? Have you dipped the moon from the sea

with the cup of night? Have you caught the rain's bow in a pool and shut it in?

This scene is performed with chorus in the show.

Go, hunt the wild jus - tice down to walk with men.

mf Poco più mosso

Have you plot - ted the high cold course of a her - on's fly - ing, Or the

thought of an old man dy - ing, Or the cov - ered la - by - rinth of

why you love where you love Or, if one love you, why your love is

met?   Not yet,   No,   not quite yet...   not

Più mosso

yet...   When the first judge sat in his place   And the mur-der-er held his breath   With

fear of death in his face,   fear of death for death.   And

all that could be said,   for or a - gainst was said,   And the

THE BIG BLACK GIANT
from *Me and Juliet*

Music by RICHARD RODGERS
Words by OSCAR HAMMERSTEIN II

LARRY:

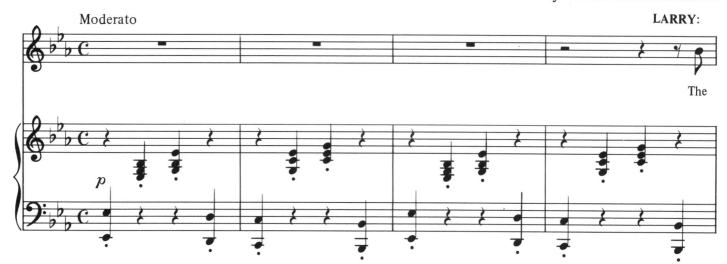

ears. _____ A big black mass Of love and pit-y And trou-bles and hopes and fears; _____ And ev-'ry night The mix-ture's dif-f'rent Al-though it may look the same. _____ To feel his way With ev-'ry mix-ture Is part of the act-or's

THAT'S THE WAY IT HAPPENS
from *Me and Juliet*

Music by RICHARD RODGERS
Words by OSCAR HAMMERSTEIN II

French fried po - ta - toes and a T bone steak.

Then a - long comes a fel - low who is quick - er than you, And he

does what you thought that you would like to do. He takes her to a bis - tro where they

give you a break With French fried po - ta - toes and a

That's the way it hap - pens,   That's the
way   it   hap - pened   to   me!

A WAND'RING MINSTREL I
from *The Mikado*

Words by W.S. GILBERT
Music by ARTHUR SULLIVAN

146

Allegro pesante, non troppo vivo (♪ = 160)

And if you call for a

song _ of the sea, We'll _ heave _ the cap - stan round, _ With a yeo heave - ho, for the

wind _ is __ free, Her an - chor's a - trip and her helm's a - lee, Hur - rah for the home - ward

bound!   To

lay a-loft in a howl-ing breeze May tick-le a lands-man's taste,   But the hap-piest hour a ___

sail - or ___ sees Is when he's down At an in - land ___ town, With his Nan - cy on his

knees, yeo - ho! And his arm ___ a - round her waist!

148

ON THE STREET WHERE YOU LIVE

from *My Fair Lady*

Words by ALAN JAY LERNER
Music by FREDERICK LOEWE

never saw a more en-chant-ing farce,

Than the mo-ment when she shouted, "Move your bloom-in' . . ."

rall.

pp
a tempo

Allegro moderato

poco rit.

p

Tempo giusto

I have of-ten walked

con tenderezza
p

* In the show Freddy is interrupted at this point. The editor suggests a chuckle here in this "stand-alone" edition of the song.

down this street be - fore; _____ But the pave - ment al - ways

stayed be - neath my feet be - fore. _____ All at once am I

sev - 'ral sto - ries high, _____ Know - ing I'm on the

street where you live. _____ Are there li - lac trees _____

the tow-er-ing feel - ing _____ Just to know _____

some - how you are near! _____ The o

- ver-pow-er-ing feel - ing _____ That an - y sec - ond you may

sud - den - ly ap - pear! _____ Peo - ple stop and stare. _____

154

KANSAS CITY
from *Oklahoma!*

Music by RICHARD RODGERS
Words by OSCAR HAMMERSTEIN II

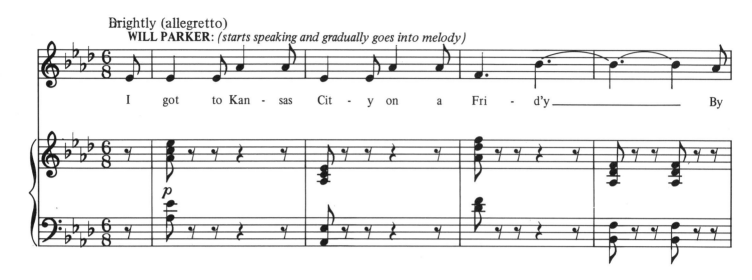

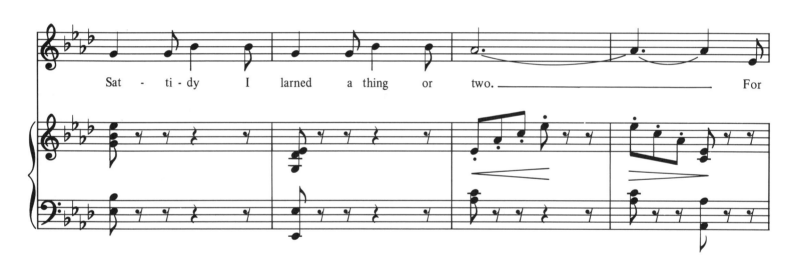

whut the mod - ren world was com - in' to! _____ I

count - ed twen - ty gas bug - gies go - in' by their - sel's

Al - most ev - 'ry time I tuck a walk _____

'Nen I put my ear to a Bell Tel - e - phone And a

strange wom - ern start - ed in to talk! _____

Refrain

Ev -'ry-thin's up to date in Kan - sas Cit - y _____ They've
Ev -'ry-thin's up to date in Kan - sas Cit - y _____ They've

mf

gone a - bout as fur as they c'n go! _____ They
gone a - bout as fur as they c'n go! _____ They

went and built a sky - scrap - er sev - en stor - ies
got a big the - ay - ter they call a bur - lee -

high _____ A - bout as high as a build - in' ort - a y
que _____ Fer fif - ty cents you c'n see a dand - y

grow. Ev - 'ry-thin's like a dream in Kan - sas
show. One of the gals was fat and pink and

Cit - y _____ It's bet - ter than a
pret - ty _____ As round a - bove as

MANY MOONS AGO

from *Once Upon a Mattress*

Music by MARY RODGERS
Words by MARSHALL BARER

find a lass Who would suit his moth-er's pride. For a

prin-cess is a del-i-cate thing, Del-i-cate and dain-ty as a

(dolce)

dra-gon fly's wing. You can re-cog-nize a la-dy by her el-e-gant air, But a

gen-u-ine prin-cess is ex-ceed-ing-ly rare.

rit.

Keep moving

On a storm-y night, to the cas-tle door, Came the
lass the prince had been wait-ing for. "I'm a prin-cess lost" quoth she. But the
queen was cool and re-mained a-loof And she said: "Per-haps, but she'll
need some proof. I'll pre-pare a test and see. I will

test her thus," the old queen said: I'll put twen-ty down-y mat-tress-

es up-on her bed And be-tween those twen-ty mat-tress-es I'll place a ti-ny pea. If that

pea dis-turbs her slum-ber, then a true prin-cess is she.

Now, the bed was soft and ex - treme - ly tall, But the dain - ty lass did - n't sleep at all. And she told them so next day. Said the queen: "My dear, if you felt that pea, Then we've proof e - nough of your roy - al - ty. Let the wed - ding mu - sic

Slowly

play." And the peo-ple shout-ed qui-et-ly: "Hoo-ray!" For a

pp

Tempo I°

prin-cess is a del-i-cate thing, Del-i-cate and dain-ty as a

dra-gon fly's wing. You can re-cog-nize a la-dy by her el-e-gant air, But a

Slowly

gen-u-ine prin-cess is ex-ceed-ing-ly rare.

rit.

I COULD WRITE A BOOK

from *Pal Joey*

Words by LORENZ HART
Music by RICHARD RODGERS

mount. _____ But my bus - y

mind is burn-ing to use what learn-ing I've got.

I won't waste an - y time, I'll strike while the i - ron is

hot. If they asked me I could write a book _____

p (melody)

About the way you walk and whis - per and look.

I could write a pre - face on how we

met, So the world would nev - er for - get.

And the sim - ple se - cret of the plot

(melody)

ALL KINDS OF PEOPLE
from *Pipe Dream*

Music by RICHARD RODGERS
Words by OSCAR HAMMERSTEIN II

Allegretto *(in 4)*

DOC:

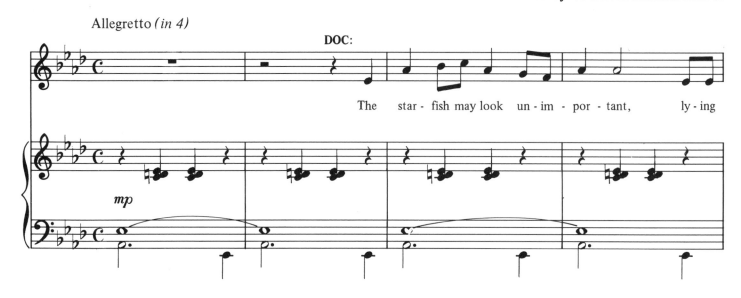

The star-fish may look un-im-por-tant, ly-ing

limp-ly on his un-der wa-ter shelf. He may look un-im-por-tant to you, But he's

In 2 *(not too fast)*

ve-ry in-ter-est-ing to him-self._____ It takes all kinds of

colla voce

(crossing hands)

174

In 2 *(not too fast)*

all kinds of peo-ple to make up a world,

All kinds of peo-ple and things._____ They

crawl on the earth, They swim in the sea, and they

fly through the sky on wings;_____

YOU'RE DEVASTATING
from *Roberta*

Words by OTTO HARBACH
Music by JEROME KERN

HUCK:

When I think of you who are, What a gem true blue you are,

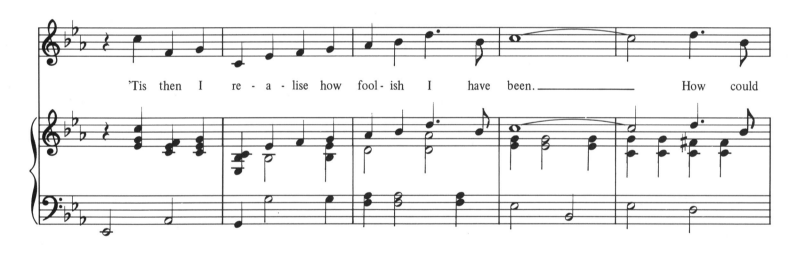

'Tis then I re-a-lise how fool-ish I have been. _____ How could

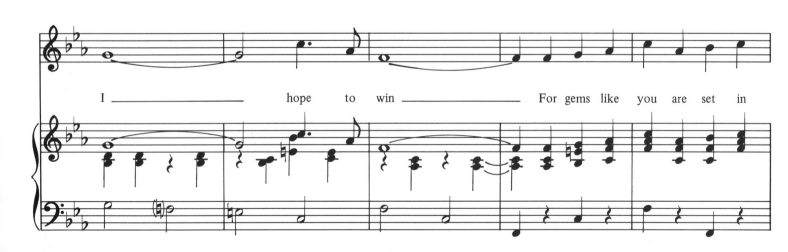

I _____ hope to win _____ For gems like you are set in

rings, That grace the hands of Kings.

You're de-vas-tat-ing, And so far a-bove me

So think of mat-ing I nev-er could dare. You could-n't

ev-er be low-ly and love me, You're much too cle-ver to

care how I care. _____ You were des - tined for pur - ple - hued

throne rooms, _____ You were fash - ioned for princ - es to

slowly

see, _____ Still, I keep dream-ing of you in my own rooms, ___

slowly

opt. 8va

___ And there you whis - per "I love you" to me. _____

THE ONLY HOME I KNOW
from *Shenandoah*

Music by GARY GELD
Words by PETER UDELL

Andante Rubato

CORPORAL:

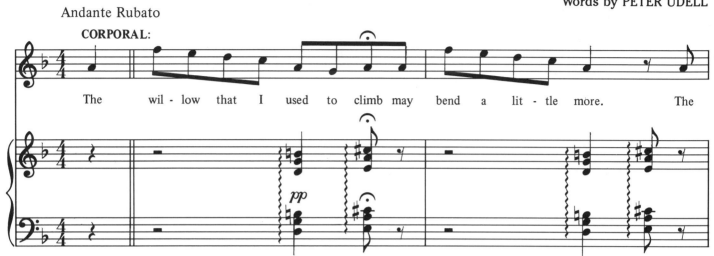

The wil-low that I used to climb may bend a lit-tle more. The

paint may all be peel-in' off the front porch and the door. No mat-ter what, I'm head-in' back and

whis-tlin' as I go.___ For bet-ter or for worse, it's still the on-ly home I know.___ The

This song is sung with chorus in the show.

penny in a wishing well, copper turned rust. I can't remember why I left or
what I hoped to find. I only know that more and more I'm back there in my mind. ___ A
fire-place, a gentle face, a warm and friend-ly glow. ___ Please let it be the way it was, The
only home I know. The only home I know. ___

YOU'VE GOT TO BE CAREFULLY TAUGHT

from *South Pacific*

Words by OSCAR HAMMERSTEIN II
Music by RICHARD RODGERS

YOUNGER THAN SPRINGTIME

from *South Pacific*

Words by OSCAR HAMMERSTEIN II
Music by RICHARD RODGERS

Lento, molto calmo

Moderate e tranquillo
CABLE:

I touch your hand And my arms grow strong_____ Like a pair of birds That burst with song_____

My eyes look down At your love - ly face

And I hold the world In my em - brace.

Young - er than Spring - time are you Soft - ter than star - light are you

pp molto legato

Warm - er then winds of June are the gen - tle lips you gave me.

Gay-er than laugh-ter are you Sweet-er than mu-sic _____ are you

An-gel and lov-er, heav-en and earth are you to me. And when your

youth and joy in-vade my arms And fill my

heart as now they do... then...

mf

Young- er than Spring- time am I Gay- er than laugh - ter am I

An - gel and lov - er, heav - en and earth am I with

you.

And when your youth and joy in - vade my

arms And fill my heart as now they do . . .

then . . . Young-er than Spring-time am I Gay-er than laugh-ter

am I An-gel and lov-er, heav-en and earth am I

with you.

LONELY HOUSE
from *Street Scene*

Words by LANGSTON HUGHES
Music by KURT WEILL

Some-times I hear a ba-by cry.

Some-times I hear a stair-case creak-ing, _____

Some-times a dis-tant tel-e-phone.

Then the qui-et set-tles down a-gain - - -

The house and I are all a-lone.

L'istesso tempo
with soft expression

Lone - ly house, lone - ly me!

Fun-ny - - with so man-y neigh - bors, How lone - ly it can

be! Oh lone - ly street! Lone - ly

town! Fun-ny - - you can be so lone - ly with all these folks a-

round. I guess there must be some - thing I don't com - pre-

FINISHING THE HAT

from *Sunday in the Park With George*

Words and Music by
STEPHEN SONDHEIM

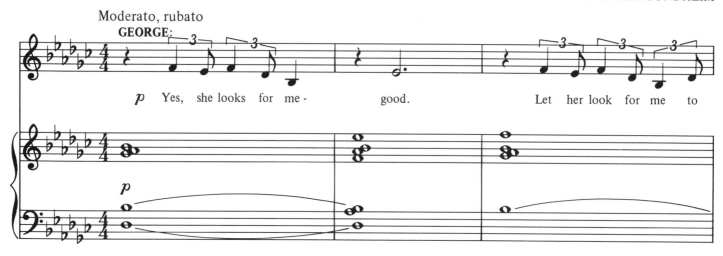

poco rall.   *a tempo, non rubato*

rea - son that they should _____   But if   an - y -bod- y could...____

sempre legato

Fin - ish - ing the   hat,   how you have to

fin - ish the hat. __   How you watch the   rest of the world from a

com - ing from the hat, stud - y - ing the

hat, en - ter - ing the world of the hat, ___

reach - ing through the world of the hat ___ like a win - dow, ___ back to

this one from that. ___ Stud - y - ing a face,

__ what I give." But the wom - an who won't wait for you knows __ that, how -

ev - er you live, __ there's a part __ of you al - ways stand ing by,

map-ping out the sky,

dim.

fin - ish - ing a hat...

Start - ing on a hat...

Fin - ish - ing a

hat...

Look, I made a hat...

poco cresc.

Where there nev - er was a

hat...

(cresc.)

f

ff

JOHANNA
from *Sweeney Todd*

Lyric and Music by STEPHEN SONDHEIM

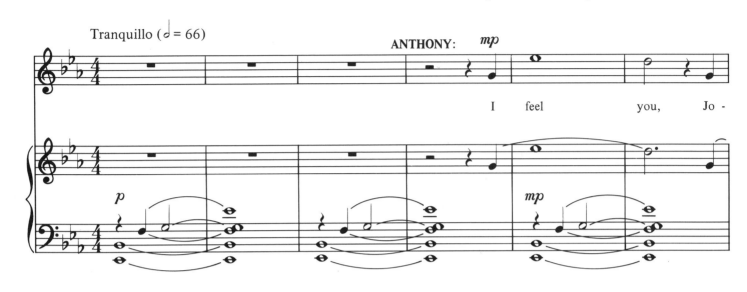

Maestoso (♩ = 66)

205

han - na! _____ I'll

steal you, Jo - han - na, I'll steal you.

Con poco moto

Do they think that walls can hide _____ you? E - ven now I'm at your win - dow.

I am in the dark be - side _____ you, Bur-ied sweet-ly in your yel-low hair. . . _____

A tempo

I feel you, Jo-han-na, And one day I'll steal you.

Till I'm with you then, I'm with you there, Sweet-ly bur-ied in your yel-low hair.

cresc. poco a poco

NOT WHILE I'M AROUND

from *Sweeney Todd*

Words and Music by
STEPHEN SONDHEIM

Demons 'll charm you with a smile For a while, But in time

Nothing can harm you, Not while I'm a round.

Not to worry, Not to worry,

I may not be smart but I ain't dumb. I can do it,

No one's gon-na hurt you, No one's gon-na dare.

Oth-ers can de-sert you, Not to wor-ry, Whis-tle, I'll be there.

De-mons 'll charm you with a smile For a while, But in time

Noth-ing's gon-na harm you, Not while I'm a-round.

LADIES IN THEIR SENSITIVITIES

from *Sweeney Todd*

Music and Words by
STEPHEN SONDHEIM

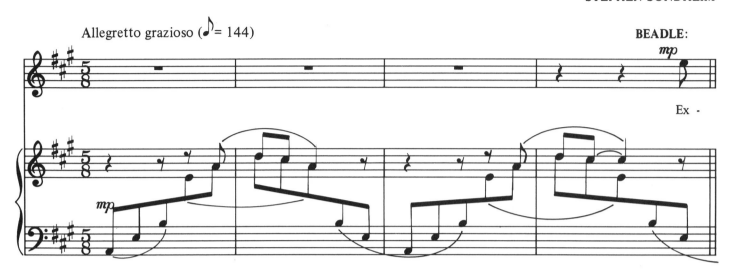

WISH YOU WERE HERE
from *Wish You Were Here*

Words and Music by
HAROLD ROME

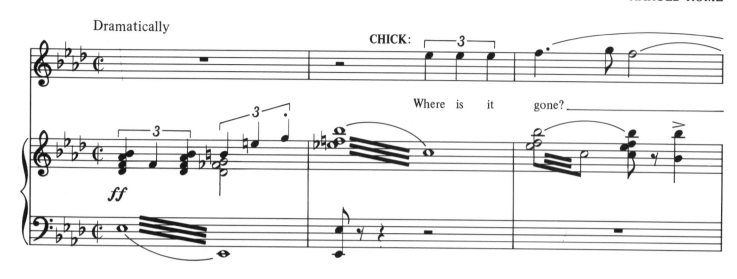

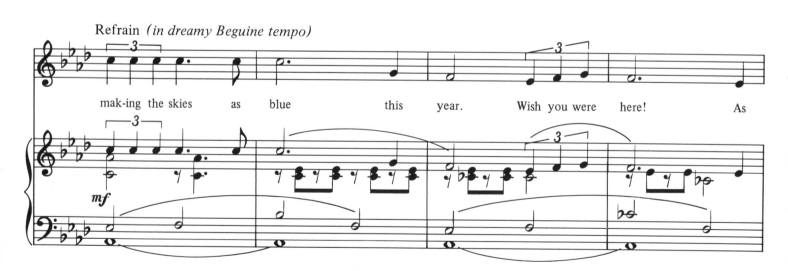

blue as they used to when you were near. Wish you were here! And the

morn-ings don't seem as new, Brand new as they did with you. Wish you were

here! Wish you were here! Wish you were here! _____ Some-one's

paint-ing the leaves all wrong this year. Wish you were

218

219

paint-ing the leaves all wrong this year. Wish you were here! And

why did the birds change their song This year? Wish you were here! They're not

shin-ing the stars as bright. They've stol-en the joy from the night. _____

Very slowly

_____ Wish you were here! Wish you were here! Wish you were here! _____

I DO NOT KNOW A DAY
I DID NOT LOVE YOU

from *Two by Two*

Words by MARTIN CHARNIN
Music by RICHARD RODGERS

Moderately slow

JAPHETH:

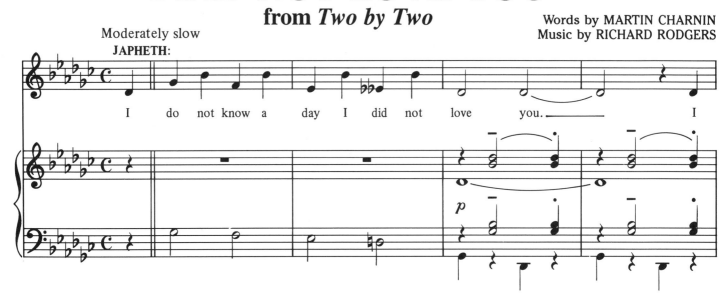

I do not know a day I did not love you. ___ I

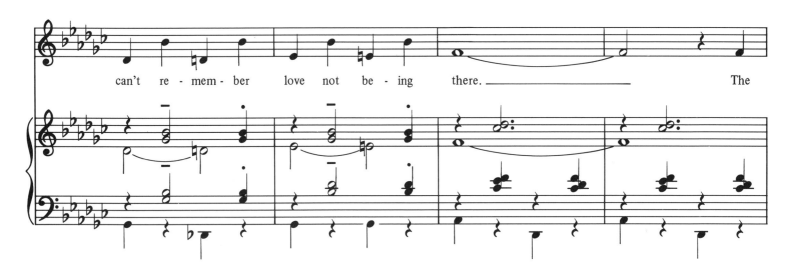

can't re-mem-ber love not be-ing there. ___ The

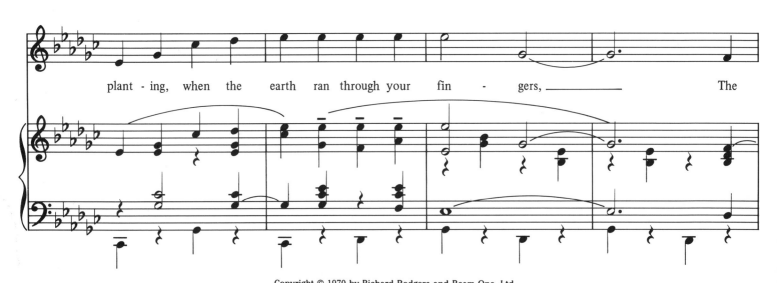

plant-ing, when the earth ran through your fin - gers, ___ The